AF008

MASSIMILIANO AFIERO

AXIS FORCES
8

WW2 AXIS
FORCES

The Axis Forces 008 - First edition November 2018 by Luca Cristini Editor for the brand Soldiershop
Cover & Art Design by soldiershop factory. ISBN code: 978-88-93273916

In merito alla specifica serie Italia storia ebook serie Ritterkreuz l'editore Luca Cristini Editore informa che non essendone l'autore ne il primo editore del materiale pervenuto dall'associazione Ritterkreuz, declina ogni responsabilità in merito al suo contenuto di testi e/o immagini e la sua correttezza. A tal proposito segnaliamo che la pubblicazione Ritterkreuz tratta esclusivamente argomenti a carattere storico-militare e non intende esaltare alcun tipo di ideologia politica presente o del passato cosi come non intende esaltare alcun tipo di regime politico del secolo precedente ed alcuna forma di razzismo.

Note editoriali dell'edizione cartacea

The Axis Forces number 8 – October 2018

Direction and editing
Via San Giorgio, 11 – 80021 AFRAGOLA (NA) -ITALY
Managing and Chief Editor: Massimiliano Afiero
Email: maxafiero@libero.it - **Website**: www.maxafiero.it

Contributors

Tomasz Borowski, Stefano Canavassi, Carlos Caballero Jurado, Rene Chavez, Carlo Cucut, Daniel Fanni, Dmitry Frolov, Antonio Guerra, Lars Larsen, Christophe Leguérandais, Eduardo M. Gil Martínez, Peter Mooney, Péter Mujzer, Ken Niewiarowicz, Erik Norling, Raphael Riccio, Marc Rikmenspoel, Charles Trang, Cesare Veronesi, Sergio Volpe.

Editorial

With this issue, we conclude our second year of publication, a satisfying achievement, always hoping to have met your interest and have contributed to the progress of historical research on the subject of voluntary formations in the Axis forces during the Second World War. For the next year, we plan to further improve our work and enrich more and more, with new and interesting articles, our and your magazine. To this end, we invite you as always to keep us in mind and send us your comments and critiques regarding our articles, so that we can meet and fulfill your requests. Thank you all for your cooperation. Let's now analyze the contents of this issue of the magazine. Let's start with the first part of an article dedicated to the Dutch Legion, richly illustrated. We continue with the biography of Johannes Göhler, officer in the SS cavalry units, with the second part of the article dedicated to the Barbarigo *battalion on the Anzio front, with the new work on the Hungarian paratroopers of our new collaborator Péter Mujzer, with an excerpt from the new Tomasz Borowski's book on the last engagements of the French volunteers of Charlemagne, the third part of the photographic reportage dedicated to the SS-Hauptsturmführer Hans-Jörg Hartmann and we close with the article on the decorations of the Dutch volunteers. Happy reading to everyone and see you in the next issue...*

Massimiliano Afiero

Contents

The Dutch Volunteer Legion	Pag. 5
Johannes Göhler, Knights Cross Holder from the 8.SS-Kav.-Division	Pag. 27
The Barbarigo Battalion on the Anzio Front, 2nd part	Pag. 33
Hungarian Airborne Operation in 1941	Pag. 42
The last battle of the Charlemagne Division	Pag. 49
SS-Hauptsturmfuhrer Hans-Jörg Hartmann, 3rd part	Pag. 60
Dutch Legion Awards	Pag. 70

For your honor and conscience! Fight Bolshevism - The *Waffen-SS* is calling you!

The Dutch Volunteer Legion
by Massimiliano Afiero

Arnold Meijer.

Anton Mussert.

The beginning of the campaign in the east called for the formation throughout Europe of volunteer legions to participate alongside the Germans in the crusade against Bolshevism. The idea of forming a legion of Dutch volunteers to fight on the Eastern Front was proposed on 28 June 1941, by the leader of the National Front (*Nationaal Front*), Arnold Meijer. Naturally, the Germans supported the idea and quickly authorized the project. When, however, Meijer learned of the direct involvement of the SS in the Legion, he abandoned the project and left the organization in the hands of Anton Mussert's NSB (*National-Socialistische Beweging*). Meijer wanted an independent national legion, while the SS wanted absolute control of all of the volunteer formations of Germanic origin. Mussert, in contrast to Meijer, guaranteed the Germans his complete support for the formation of the Legion and above all with respect to the recruiting campaign. The head of the NSB saw the Legion as the embryo of a new Dutch army. On 10 July 1941, the *Reichskommisar* in Holland, Arthur Seyss-Inquart, officially announced the establishment of the Dutch Legion, the *Freiwilligen Legion Niederlande* (originally designated the *Freiwilligen Verband Niederlande*). Lieutenant General H.A. Seyffardt, ex-Chief of Staff of the Dutch Army, was chosen as its first commander. The following day, the recruiting campaign began throughout the country, promoted by the local chapters of the NSB party. Mussert invited all of the members of the NSB itself to join the Legion to set the example; many young people signed up, especially those who were members of the *Weerbaarheidsafdeling*, who went on to join the 1,400 Dutch volunteers of the disbanded *Nordwest* Regiment. From nearby Flanders, some Flemish volunteers arrived who preferred to enlist in the Dutch Legion rather than in the Flemish Legion. It should be noted that some Dutch citizens of Asian origin who had emigrated to Holland from the far-off colonies of the Dutch East Indies were also accepted into the ranks. The officer cadre of the Legion was drawn from Dutch officers who were already serving with the *Westland* and *Wiking* regiments.

Lieutenant General H.A. Seyffardt.

Dutch volunteers marching in the streets of Hague, summer 1941.

Dutch volunteers in the summer of 1941 applying to join the Dutch Volunteer Legion.

Dutch volunteers departing for training, October 1941.

Departing for training

Around mid-October 1941, the volunteers were transferred to the *Truppenübungsplatz* at Arys (in Eastern Prussia, now in Poland and known as Orzysz), where their training began under the direction of demanding German instructors. The ability of the young Dutch volunteers to adapt to the discipline and strict German training system was not easy and there were numerous incidents between the ausbilders (instructors) and the volunteers. There were also several defections, among those that of the elderly General Seyffardt, who tendered his resignation when he realized that the Legion was to become a combat unit of the *Waffen SS*. Command of the Legion thus passed to a German officer, *SS-Oberführer* Otto Reich, who had previously commanded the *SS-Totenkopfstandarte 4 Ostmark* and later the *SS-Totenkopfstandarte 2 Brandenburg*.

Otto Reich.

The swearing-in ceremony for Dutch volunteers.

Dutch volunteers during training at the Arys camp, December 1941.

In early January 1942, the Legion completed its training and was declared officially ready to be transferred to the front. The *SS-Freiwilligen Legion Niederlande*, with a strength of about three thousand volunteers, was organized with three infantry battalions, each with four companies, plus a thirteenth company with infantry support guns and a fourteenth anti-tank company.

About the uniforms, from the beginning, the Dutch legionnaires wore the normal *Waffen SS* uniform with a special collar tab, the runic sign of the wolf hook (*Wolfsangel*), which they wore on the uniform lapel. There were two styles of this tab: horizontal or vertical.

Dutch volunteers. Note on their *Waffen-SS* uniform, the special collar tab, the sleeve patch with the Dutch national colors and the cuff title with the inscription "*Frw.Legion Niederlande*".

The swearing-in ceremony for Dutch volunteers, October 1941.

In addition, on their *Waffen SS* uniform, the Dutch volunteers also wore the *Prinsevlag* (the orange, white and blue flag) which was the sleeve patch with the Dutch national colors, also produced in various styles.

In November 1941, the Dutch legion was authorized to wear a cuff title with the German inscription "*Frw.Legion Niederlande*" (Dutch Volunteer Legion).

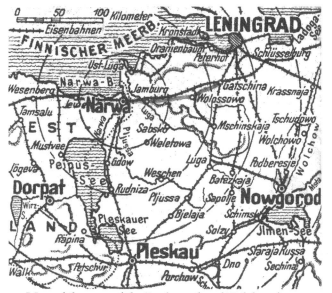

Map of the area of the Leningrad and Volchov front.

January 1942: *SS-Stubaf.* Richard Pöhle, with two officers of his battalion, the *I./Niederlande* (NA).

A Dutch volunteer in his defensive position, January 1942.

Volchov front

Once training had been completed, the Dutch volunteers were transferred by sea from Danzig to Libau, around the middle of January 1942. From there, the Legion was moved by train to the front at Volchov, north of Lake Ilmen, smack in the middle of the Soviet winter counteroffensive. The Dutch volunteers were deployed to trenches dug in the snow at Selo Gora, on the Volchov River, in front of the sacred city of Novgorod south of Leningrad, taking over the front lines from the 90th Infantry Regiment of the German 20th Motorized Infantry Division under *Generalmajor* Erich Jaschke. The Dutch Legion was initially subordinated to *Generalmajor* Jaschke's division, engaged in various security operations in the rear area of the 18th Army. The Dutch volunteers took up positions in a series of entrenchments between the cities of Tschudovo and Novgorod, with the mission of defending the western bank of the Volchov River. In that area, the Soviets had for days been exerting massive pressure in an attempt to establish a bridgehead on the western bank of the river. But even before dealing with the Soviets, the Dutch volunteers had to defend themselves against the terrible weather conditions, from the cold and the ice, which caused the transfer of the first casualties to the field hospitals. Covering the Legion's flanks, in addition to units of the 20th Division, there were also units from the 254th Division (commanded by *Generalleutnant* Walter Behschnitt). The Dutch, along with other German units, constituted the *Kampfgruppe Jaschke*, named after its commanding general.

A Legion defensive position on the Volchov front.

A Legion patrol on a scouting mission.

Dutch legionaires on the Volchov front, February 1942.

The 1st Battery of the *SS-Polizei Division* (*1./Polizei-Artillerie-Regiment*) commanded by *Hauptmann* Hellmuth Vogel had been transferred to the Gusi-Selo Gora corridor. This unit remained in this area in support of the Dutch Legion until the middle of April. In early February 1942, the leader of the NSB, Anton Mussert, accompanied by the leader of the *Weerbaarheidsafdeling* Zondervan, made a visit to the Legion bringing gift packages to the volunteers and above all a load of winter clothing to protect them better from the bitter cold of Russia. During the visit an official ceremony was also organized during which the first Iron Crosses were presented to the Dutch volunteers who had distinguished themselves in combat.

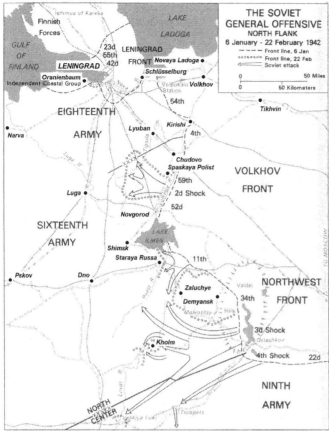

A *MG-34* position on the Volchov front, 1942.

The Soviets attack

On 10 February 1942, in the context of the great Russian counteroffensive along the Volchov, the Dutch positions were among those that were hit, first by the heavy preliminary enemy artillery shelling and then by the direct attack of infantry and tanks. The Soviet high command sent experienced Siberian units who were well suited to fighting in the cold and in the snow, in the first wave. The forward positions were overrun, but the Germans reacted promptly and carried out fierce counterattacks in which the Dutch volunteers were also engaged. The orders were clear, to hold the positions at all costs. The Dutch volunteers were able to stem the spirited enemy attack, although they paid a high price in blood. On 11 February, the Legion's II Battalion was engaged along the Gora-Gusi road; the Soviets had set up a road block and the Dutch were called upon to eliminate it. As the Dutch column was nearing the village of Gusi it fell into an enemy ambush and was attacked by a strong and battle-hardened Soviet unit, losing six men. The Soviets also suffered significant losses and also had three of their number taken prisoner. The Soviet offensive continued until the end of February, without however breaking through the German resistance. During the days that followed, the Legion was engaged in destroying pockets of Soviet resistance in the area around the villages of Pjatilipy and Gorenka; the forested nature of the area made operations more difficult, but the sweep operation was ultimately successful, with many enemy bunkers having been destroyed by the Dutchmen only after having engaged in violent close-quarter fighting. Having returned to their defensive positions and finding themselves under continuous Soviet artillery fire, the volunteers had to further fortify their own positions, building bunkers and entrenchments.

Award of the first Iron Crosses to Dutch volunteers following the fighting at Selo Gora, in the presence of Zondervan, wearing the German uniform and the rank of *Untersturmführer*.

A transport column of the Legion.

Beginning in January 1942, the legionnaires were also engaged in operations against partisan units, conducting many reconnaissance patrols and several anti-partisan sweeps. The fighting around Gorenka was especially hard, where the Dutch volunteers had to defend themselves against massive attacks by well-armed and battle-hardened partisan units. After having wrested the forest north of Selo Gora from the Soviets and having eliminated pockets of enemy resistance on both sides of the railway line, the Legion was mentioned in the official *Wehrmacht* bulletin for the first time on 4 March 1942: "...*North of Lake Ilmen, the Dutch Legion distinguished itself particularly in combat...*".

For the entire month of March, Soviet pressure continued to be increasingly stronger; living conditions for the legionnaires accordingly continued to grow worse.

A Dutch Legion patrol returning from a reconnaissance mission behind enemy lines.

Two photos from Dutch Legion's trenches on the Leningrad front in the spring of 1942.

The seasonal thaw had transformed the battlefield into an immense quagmire; the trenches had been filled with mud. Under these tragic conditions, the Dutchmen had to continue to defend themselves against enemy attacks. The 1220th Regiment of the 366th Division and the 1002nd of the 305th Siberian divisions, attacked the Dutch positions unsuccessfully several times.

From 1 April 1942, the Dutch were temporarily put under command of *SS-Ostubaf.* Arved Theurermann, due to the momentary absence of *SS-Oberführer* Reich. During one frigid night in early April, about two Soviet platoons infiltrated the village of Gusi. The enemy penetration was quickly eliminated thanks to the exemplary cooperation between elements of the Dutch Legion and *1./Polizei-Artillerie-Regiment*, after furious close-quarter fighting. On 6 April, the Soviets returned to attack the Dutch positions, preceding their infantry assault with a massive artillery barrage and heavy bombing by aircraft. Once the maelstrom of fire was over, a thousand Soviet infantrymen charged against the trenches defended by the Dutch; the fire from machine guns and mortars once again stopped the advance of the Soviet hordes, who were finally forced to withdraw.

A Dutch sniper on the Volchov front, March 1942.

Dutch SS Volunteer on the radio in his trench, 1942.

A Dutch soldier on the lookout near Leningrad.

Other attacks followed, but the Dutch managed to maintain a firm hold on their positions. At the end of April, the Soviets came back again to attack the village of Gusi, which had been abandoned a few days earlier by elements of the *Polizei*. But although by themselves, the Dutch managed to throw back the Soviets. The Volchov front, thanks in part to the actions of the Dutch volunteers, was able to hold fast. With the beginning of the German offensive, the Legion was engaged in fighting aimed at eliminating the Volchov pocket, in which the Soviet forces under Geneal Vlasov had been surrounded. On 13 January, Vlasov had crossed the Volchov River with numerically superior forces with the objective of lifting the siege of Leningrad. Ultimately, his Second Shock Army and parts of the 52nd and 59th Soviet Armies had been destroyed; the Soviets suffered the loss of more than a hundred thousand men dead and wounded, and tens of thousands taken prisoner. The Dutch volunteers themselves were credited with capturing 3,500 Soviet prisoners in addition to large quantities of weapons, ammunition and equipment. Fighting in the Selo Gora area continued until June 1942, after which the survivors of the Legion were pulled back from the front lines for a period of rest and reorganization. The Dutch volunteers were awarded fully thirty two Iron Crosses First Class and 158 Second Class. In a proclamation issued on 28 June 1942 by General Lindemann, commander of the German 18th Army, the author of Vlasov's defeat, he recognized officially the contribution made by all of the foreign volunteers to the victory on the Leningrad front: *"Soldiers of the Army. On 13 January, the enemy crossed the Volchov with numerically superior forces forcing back our defensive front. His objective was the liberation of Leningrad. In five and a half months of bloody battles and unimaginably difficult conditions, our courage and our persistence have completely frustrated the enemy's intentions.*

SS-Stubaf. **Arved Theuermann awarding decorations to the Dutch legionaires who had distinguished themselves in action, Spring 1942.**

SS-Obersturmbannführer **Fitzthum.**

The remnants of the Soviet Second Shock Army and large portions of the Soviet 52nd and 59th Armies have been destroyed. All units of the Army have participated in these battles. Spaniards, Dutchmen and Flemings fought side by side with units of the army and of the Waffen SS…*".*

The battle for Krasnoje-Selo

In June 1942, the Dutch Legion was subordinated tactically to the 2nd SS Infantry Brigade, commanded by *SS-Brigadeführer* Gottfried Klingemann. On 15 July 1942, *SS-Obersturmbannführer* Fitzthum assumed command of the Legion, replacing the unpopular *Oberführer* Reich, who had never managed to gain the sympathy of the Dutch volunteers. Once the sweeps in the Volchov area had been completed, the Dutch volunteers were engaged in keeping watch over the Leningrad-Novgorod railway line, along with the *285.Sicherungs-Division* of *Generalleutnant* Wolfgang Edler Herr and Freiherr von Plotho.

Soldiers of the Dutch Legion of the *Waffen-SS* in a position at a railway embankment on the Eastern front near the Lake Ilmen.

A war correspondent with the Dutch Legion.

Waffen-SS **Officier speaks to one of his MG man on the Leningrad front, Summer 1942.**

At the end of July the Legion, still attached to the 2nd SS Brigade, was transferred further to the north to take part in the siege operations against Leningrad. On 24 July 1942, the Legion had about six hundred men still fit for combat; specifically, 16 officers, 79 NCOs and 478 men out of a nominal strength of more than a thousand soldiers. The difference between the nominal strength and the effective strength was attributable to the great number of personnel who were convalescing in various field hospitals.

Dutch volunteers on the Leningrad front, Summer 1942.

SS-Unterscharführer.

Dutch trench position on the Leningrad front. The sign incorporated both the German and Dutch SS Symbols and the Dutch SS motto *'Hou en Trou'*.

After about a month of relative calm in the trenches around Leningrad, the Legion was withdrawn from the front lines in preparation for Operation *Nordlicht* (North Light) which called for a final assault against the city. The date for the beginning of the offensive was set for 14 August 1942, but the Germans were preempted by a massive Soviet counteroffensive south of Lake Ladoga. As a consequence of postponement *sine die* of the planned offensive the Dutch volunteers were once again transferred south of Leningrad, this time in the area of Krasnoje-Selo and were kept busy fighting off new Soviet attacks. The ensuing encounters along the front south of Leningrad passed into history as the *"First Battle of Lake Ladoga"*.

Beginning on 2 September 1942, a new independent combat group was formed within the 2nd SS Brigade, which took the name of its commander, *SS-Obersturmbannführer* Fitzthum, and which consisted of the Dutch Legion, the Norwegian Legion, and the 19th and 20th

Latvian battalions. The units of the *Kampfgruppe* were engaged mainly in bitter defensive fighting until December 1942. On 4 December 1942, the Dutch volunteers were called upon to repel yet another enemy attack against their positions; a Soviet assault force of about six hundred men was unleashed against the *I.Battalion* of the Legion and many of the Soviets were able to pass through the lines.

Dutch volunteers in winter uniforms ready to combat, 1942.　　**An *MG-34* troop in a trench.**

German soldiers take cover behind damaged Soviet tanks.

The *Kampfgruppe* responded with a counterattack using Norwegian and Dutch units to reestablish the former defensive line. About 350 Soviet soldiers were killed and 42 taken prisoner, while *Kampfgruppe* losses were 30 killed, 66 wounded and three missing in action.

The Second Battle of Lake Ladoga

In early January 1943, the Soviet launched yet another offensive south of Lake Ladoga with the intention of easing the pressure on Leningrad, known as the *"Second Battle of Lake Ladoga"*. The Norwegians and Dutch were called upon to repel numerous Soviet armored attacks, during which the anti-tank detachments were particularly hard-pressed. During an attack by an enemy armored formation, a young 19-year old volunteer, Gerardus Leonardus Mooyman of the *14.Panzerjäger Kompanie*, was able to destroy a total of thirteen Soviet tanks with his gun during a single day. *Sturmmann* Mooyman was later awarded the Knight's Cross.

Norwegian anti-tank crew on the Leningrad front, 1943.

Dutch artillery in action!

Johannes-Gerardus Leonardus Mooyman.

In March 1943, the Legion passed under tactical command of the 4th SS Armored Grenadier Regiment *Polizei*. Following a series of bloody engagements, attacks and withdrawals, in April 1943, the Legion was down to only 20% of its initial effective strength figure.

Johannes Gerardus Leonardus Mooyman

Born on 23 September 1923 in Apeldoorn in the Dutch province of Gelderland. At the age of 19 he enlisted in the *Waffen SS*, and as did many of his countrymen he joined the ranks of *SS-Freiwilligen-Standarte Nordwest*, which was the regiment created by Himmler in which to gather the Flemish, Dutch, and in general all of the volunteers who were of Germanic stock. After completing training as a *Panzerjäger* (anti-tank gunner) at Hilvorsum in Holland, he was transferred to the *SS-Freiwilligen-Legion Nederland*. He began his career at the front as a message runner, despite the fact that he had been trained as an anti-tank gunner. On 15 January 1943, at the front in Leningrad, some batteries of the Dutch Legion (*14.Panzerjäger Kompanie* commanded by *Ostuf.* Walter Diener) and of the Norwegian Legion (*14.Pak Kompanie*) were temporarily detached from the 2nd SS Brigade, by direct order of *SS-Brigadeführer* Klingemann and assigned to reinforce *SS-Polizei Regiment 16* (*Oberstleutnant der Schutzpolizei* Kemper). On 21 January 1943, another battery consisting of two *Pak* guns of the Norwegian 14th Company, commanded by *Unterscharführer* Hans Haug, along with *Panzerjäger* from the Dutch Legion was assigned to another German unit, the *170.Infanterie Division* (*Generalleutnant* Erwin Sander), which was defending the railway hub of Mga, near Schlüsselburg.

The crew of a *Pak 35/36* anti-tank gun prepare their gun for action.　　　A Dutch legionnaire.

Dutch volunteers marching to their new positions.

A team effort is untertaken to move a 3.7cm PaK 35/36.

When they began their move to the front, the Norwegian and Dutch volunteers knew only that their destination was the village of Mga. They also knew that south of the Neva River a battle was raging. When they reached Mga they found the village overflowing with German reinforcements. The news that *"foreigners"* had arrived spread swiftly and they were given a very warm welcome. Soon after, orders came to begin the march. Guide personnel accompanied the soldiers outside the village along the road called the Burma Road, only because it led to a Soviet station called *Rangun* (Rangoon)! Under the light of the moon, the Norwegian and Dutch volunteers passed in front of the German artillery positions under incessant shelling by Soviet batteries. The capable German gunners, all of whom had been killed, were still next to their guns. The march continued until dawn, at which time the fire of mortars and heavy artillery began, soon followed by fire from the terrible *Katyusha* rocket launchers.

German soldiers examine a knocked out *KV-1* heavy tank on the Leningrad front, 1943.

The *5cm PaK38* has been fitted with quite oversized skis in order to enhance his mobility.

For four times the volunteers were forced to seek shelter to escape from the storm of Soviet fire. The Norwegians were the first to occupy forward positions. At the same moment in which the enemy tried to break through a gap that had been created in the German defensive line, the first Soviet tanks made their appearance. Soviet artillery began to shell the Norwegian positions, but to no effect. Other Soviet tanks were knocked out by Norwegian anti-tank fire, completely halting any attempt by the enemy to break through in the Rangun sector. The Dutch message runner Gerardus Mooyman was not, however, happy with his job assignment within the Legion. He was furious that he was still a simple runner rather than an anti-tank gunner. His repeated requests to his commander had fallen on deaf ears. Nevertheless, he decided to try yet again. But once again his commander was laconic, saying: *"You are beginning to get on my nerves"*. Mooyman remained calm and a few days later his wish was granted. In fact, following the heavy losses suffered by the anti-tank company, replacements were requested from all units of the Legion. Mooyman, with his training as an anti-tank gunner, was thus one of the first to be transferred to the company, with the position of gun commander (*Geschutzführer*). During the night of 30 January, the Dutch *Panzerjägers* Närger and Mooyman took up positions east of Mga. They were only eight hundred meters apart from each other.

A 7.5cm *PaK 97/38*, based on the 5cm *PaK 38* carriage on the Leningrad front, 1943.

Soviet tanks attacking German positions, February 1943.

The main aid station and the regimental command post were located between the two positions. It was not until dawn that they were able to have a clear view of the battlefield in front of their guns. On one side there was a thick forest while on the other side was a sort of passage about thirty meters wide through which the Soviets would certainly attempt to pass. From early morning, enemy machine gun fire hit the German positions incessantly. Suddenly, Mooyman spotted movement from the forest. He took his scope, slowly scanned the terrain, and saw about a dozen Soviet tanks with infantry following behind them advancing towards his position. There wasn't a moment to lose! The Soviets intended to pass right in front of his *Pak*. Mooyman had the gun loaded, continuing in the meantime to carefully monitor the enemy's movements. When the first Soviet tank entered into his field of vision, he gave the order to fire. The first round quickly hit its target, raising an infernal racket. Another round was fired while the first tank was in flames. Another tank turned and backtracked to escape the Dutch fire. The Soviet infantry then began to fire on the *Pak* crew, who continued to fire against the Soviet tanks, heedless of the bullets whistling past them.

An anti-tank crew in action on the Leningrad front, 1943.　　**Soviet infantry and armor.**

German soldiers examine a knocked out *KV-1* heavy tank.

After having hit another tank, the gun jammed unexpectedly, as a round had become stuck in the breech. Gunner Ruiter came up with an idea, even though it may have seemed stupid as well as dangerous. He jumped from his position and grabbed a heavy branch. He very calmly began to bang violently on the *Pak* with the branch, knowing full well that the banging could blow up the gun and himself along with it. However, his efforts finally paid off and the gun was able to resume firing. The Dutch anti-tank gunners stopped only after they had destroyed another four tanks and having damaged yet a further four. In the face of such determination the Soviet infantry also opted to pull back.

An anti-tank gun ready to fire, Leningrad front 1943. Only two Soviet tanks managed to break through the Dutch positions, but they were quickly knocked out with hand grenades. That day the Soviets had had enough.

German defensive position on the Leningrad front, 1943.

An anti-tank defensive position with a piece of 37mm.

A grenadier with his rifle and a destroyed enemy tank.

The next day however they resumed the attack, preceded by a massive barrage by their artillery. At six in the morning of 31 January 1943, First Gunner Närger was alert at his position. The Soviets were approaching him rapidly. Närger opened fire with high explosive shells in order to eliminate the massed Soviet infantry. Two hours of close-quarter combat action between the German and Soviet infantry ensued. The Germans, who were heavily outnumbered, were finally forced to withdraw. Närger was now by himself, thirty meters from the forward line of combat! His anti-tank position became a center of resistance by default. The Soviets tried to avoid his fire, advancing on his flank under cover of the forest. Two light anti-tank guns belonging to the same Dutch company, situated to the right and left of Närger, were destroyed. There were, however, five mortars in action to his left. When they had run out of ammunition, the mortar crews reached the Dutch anti-tank positions and continued to fight with their rifles. In the meantime, Second Gunner Kortenbach had been wounded. Närger assigned one of the ex-mortar men to replace him, but his new gunner was also hit by Soviet fire shortly afterwards, and the same fate was suffered by the next replacement as well. The machine gun covering the anti-tank gun was alone in firing against the Soviets. There was an urgent need for men. Between nine and ten in the morning ammunition also ran out. The last two rounds were held back in order to destroy the anti-tank gun itself. Panzerjägers and grenadiers gathered together around the guns with their rifles in their hands. A German assault gun arrived from the rear as reinforcement, but after having fired a couple of rounds, quickly pulled back.

A machine gun crewman awaits the order to move forward. A *StuG.III* covers his unit's advance.

SS troops utilise blocks of snow for a defensive position.

Kortenbach, wounded in one arm but still able to walk, went to look for ammunition. *SS-Sturmmann* Schaufeli accompanied him. Despite the heavy enemy fire, the pair, after having found a small cart, managed to go back and forth three times, each time carrying nine rounds. During the second trip, Schaufeli was wounded in the legs. *SS-Sturmmann* Eklenz saw to the resupply of ammunition for Mooyman's gun. This enabled the two Dutch anti-tank guns to resume their fire. The Dutch battery commander, *SS-Oberscharführer* Weide, was wounded while attempting to conduct a visual reconnaissance near Närger's position.

German troops preparing to use their *PaK 35/36*.

Närger remained alone with his gunner Stevelmanns to man his *Pak*. Ammunition ran out once again, and there were only about a dozen hand grenades left for their final defense. The Soviet emerged from the forest barely forty meters from their position. *"Whichever of us is the last left standing will destroy the gun, understood?"* shouted Närger. When all seemed lost, in the midst of the din of battle, he suddenly heard the roar of an engine at his shoulders. He raised his head and carefully looked behind: *"Why, it's Bochy !".* Bochy was the Dutch motorcycle courier. His *sidecar* was full of ammunition and he had come through at full speed in the midst of explosions and under fire from the Soviets. Now the Dutch Panzerjägers could resume their fire once again. Around noontime another motorcycle appeared. This time it was the commander who was shuttling between the two anti-tank guns commanded by Närger and Mooyman. He had his pockets full of chocolate bars for his men. Because of a round that exploded nearby, Närger had temporarily lost his hearing, which meant that he was unable to understand anything that his company commander said to him. Around evening, several platoons of German infantry reached the gun positions, managing to reestablish a defensive line. *SS-Obersturmführer* Diener had to appoint a new commander, as *Oberscharführer* Weide had deserted, and his choice fell upon *SS-Sturmmann* Feldt, who had already led a combat group from the same company. Feldt was only nineteen years old, but he was a strong and resolute young man, and it seemed that nothing ever caused him to lose his calm demeanor. Owing to the success achieved against the Soviet tanks, both the Dutch and the Norwegians began to be considered as heroes by the German soldiers. When the men of the other units passed by their positions they greeted them in a friendly manner and while food was being served, the cook arrived to say *"…Ah, it's you. Help yourselves to whatever you want!".* Naturally, after the verbal comments, awards also were given. *SS-Sturmmann* Närger was the first to receive the Iron Cross First Class. A dozen other Dutch volunteers were awarded the Second Class; among them were Mooyman, Ruiter, Stevelmanns, Feldt, Schaufeli, Kortenbach, Bruinsvel and Erklenz. No one had expected that it would end like this. In the depths of their hearts they felt very proud of themselves. The words of a German *Panzerjäger* were emblematic, who while smiling, said to them: *"You, a handful of men, come here and in three days knock out more enemy tanks than we did throughout the entire campaign!".*

Bibliography

M. Afiero, "*23.SS-Freiwilligen-Panzergrenadier-Division Nederland*", Ass. Culturale Ritterkreuz
M. Afiero, "*The 23rd Waffen SS Vol.Pz.Gr.Div. Nederland*", Schiffer Publishing (U.S.A.)
Charles Trang, "*Dictionnaire de la Waffen SS, volume 4*", Heimdal Editions

Johannes Göhler
Knights Cross Holder from the 8.SS-Kavallerie Division
by Peter Mooney

SS-Obersturmführer **Göhler.**

Göhler with camouflage uniform.

Born in Bishofswerde in 1918, he was a member of the *Hitler Youth* from the start of September 1933 until early November 1936. He joined the *SS* on the 9th of November 1936 and was assigned the SS number 310 963. He initially served within the *Allgemeine-SS*, but in early April 1937 moved to the *Totenkopfverband* and served with *'Oberbayern'* until 1939. He took part in the actions in Austria and the Sudetenland prior to the outbreak of the war. From September 1939, he is listed as serving with the *SS-Replacement Battalion 'Ost'* and holding the appointment of *SS-Stabscharführer*. He was sent to the officer school at Braunschweig from the start of August 1940 until the end of February 1941. He was posted to the *3.Kompanie, SS-Reiter Regiment 1* from the start of March and whilst there, was promoted to *SS-Untersturmführer* on the 20th of April. He was in the role of Platoon Leader for a mortar platoon. He went into Russia with this unit in mid-1941 and whilst there, earned the Second Class Iron Cross on the 2nd of October 1941. From mid-January 1942 he was moved to the post of Regimental *Adjutant* and within a couple of days was approved for the First Class Iron Cross. He was promoted to *SS-Obersturmführer* in mid-March 1942. At the start of May he took over command of the *4.Kompanie, SS-Reiter Regiment 1*. This was the same day that he was awarded the General Assault Badge. The Russian Front Medal followed in mid-August, with the Wound Badge in Black coming in mid-December 1942. He continued to lead the *4.Kompanie* throughout 1943 and in late August, conducted actions that led to him being recommended for the Knight's Cross to the Iron Cross. The recommendation was written by his Regimental Commander, Gustav Lombard, on the 5th of September and countersigned by Fegelein the following day, it reads as follows:

"SS-Obersturmführer *Göhler, who has already proved himself outstanding in the winter fighting against Russia, especially distinguished himself on the 29.8.1943 through special boldness and decisiveness. The Regiment stood in defense on the railway line from Nowo Berezkij-Taranowka against a numerically superior, heavily armed enemy. The remnants of the 4.Squadron, under the leadership of* Obersturmführer Göhler, *stood on the open northern flank and had already held off two attacks by the enemy under heavy artillery fire.*

On the 29.8.43, the last reserve of the Regiment was already exhausted and Göhler fought one after another, apparently tactically hopeless fight. The overall risk was high, but the 293. Infantry Division *was expected to arrive the next day. They were expected to close the gap that has opened several kilometers wide between the* SS-Kavallerie Division *and the* 6.Panzer Division.

At 16:00 hours, the Russians attacked simultaneously in the north and east, after 2 hours of heavy supporting fire, beginning with the positions of Schwadron Göhler. From the north, an enemy Battalion of 500 men attacked with strong fire tactics from the middle. At 17:20 hours they fell tenfold upon the position of the Schwadron of 43 men. In a desperate one-and-a-half hour, close-quarter fight, the enemy was forced to retreat leaving over 100 dead, the Russians not being able to win. However, as a result of this fight, the Schwadron was physically exhausted. Göhler saw the enormous threat from this, however, he knew that their fate had decisive meaning. He knew that they had to hold their ground as the cornerstone of the line held by the SS-Kavallerie Division. The Russians launched a further attack through the maize field at Passiki, around which the rest of Battalion where positioned. Göhler recognized the impossibility of their defense and he used the last of his men to launch a new triumphant

Göhler with the Knight's Cross.

attack. *He sent a message to the Regiment, which was involved in its' own heavy defensive fight:* 'I order you to place all heavy weapons behind me on the map'. *He screamed to his men,* 'The Russians are already running, hurrah, hurrah', *and attacked themselves with less than 40 men against 600 Russians located 200m before the maize field. A bloodbath ensued under the Russians, with a new Battalion flowing through the remainder of the first Battalion.*

SS-Obersturmführer Göhler.

An autographed photo of *SS-Ostuf.* Johannes Göhler sent to myself, following our car journey in 2000.

In this moment they encountered one Sturmgeschütze from the Regiment, leading a short push forwards, so Göhler and 16 men jumped on one and were able to pursue the enemy a few hundred metres more. The second enemy Battalion suffered hundreds of losses. However, the enemy was struck with no leaders, were no longer in a position to prepare violent reconnaissance against the troops at this cornerstone. The closing of the gap was achieved in the evening with the arrival of the 293. Infantry Division, without meeting any further enemy action".

This recommendation was approved less than two weeks later, on the 17th of September 1943. He also was awarded the German Cross in Gold on the 26th of September 1943, followed by a promotion to *SS-Hauptsturmführer* on the 9th of November the same year. He became *SS-Gruppenführer* Hermann Fegelein's *Adjutant* at the Führer Headquarters in the final week of August 1944. That was following a heavy wound he received around the Warsaw area, which removed him from frontline service and the prospect of returning was not on the horizon, due to those wounds. In letters that he wrote to his wife around that time, he found his new appointment a welcome change from the lack of activity he was forced to endure, whilst he was recovering. He also wrote that this appointment meant more to him than the award of Knight's Cross. His move there coincided with the birth of his daughter, who had also been in the Warsaw area, but was moved towards Breslau, due to the uprising. His letters detail his first face to face introduction with Adolf Hitler, and the impact that honour had upon him. His work days were long and went on into the early hours. He quickly had daily contact with the Fuhrer and the impact on his career due to that close proximity to the Fuhrer was not lost on Göhler. He had access to the top-level meetings regarding the progress of the war on all fronts, and he found that in itself, very informative and educational, as a soldier. On the occasion of his 26th birthday, he had personal congratulations from Hitler. He was moving in the circles of the top leaders and commanders within the Third Reich, from Himmler to Jodl, Hitler to Bormann; a world away from his frontline experiences.

Left photo, Johannes Göhler pictured here alongside some of his *SS-Kavallerie* Kameraden. From left to right: Siegfried Korth (later Knight's Cross holder 1945), Hans-Georg von Charpentier (with Knight's Cross), Gustav Lombard (with Knight's Cross), Johannes Gohler (with Knight's Cross and large foot bandage!) and Anton Vandieken (later Knight's Cross holder 1944). Right photo, Göhler in a formal studio setting with all of his awards.

SS-Hstuf. Göhler seen taking part in a parade, circa 1944.

He received a further promotion to *SS-Sturmbannführer* on the 21st of December 1944 and also spent a pleasant Christmas in this company. He received personal gifts from Fegelein, Guderian and others. He remained there until the 24th of April 1945, when he was part of a small contingent sent from Berlin to the Berghof, to help oversee preparations for defence there. He therefore, was not caught up in the final fighting for Berlin, but he was witness to other significant occurrences as the Third Reich era came to a close. He accompanied the heavily pregnant wife of Hermann Fegelein, and Eva Braun's sister to this area. Part of that interaction gave him a personal assignment, from her, to personally oversee the destruction of almost 200 private letters between Adolf Hitler and Eva Braun. They located themselves around Fischhorn Castle, around 50 miles south of Berchtesgaden. Also there at that time, was Fegelein's brother, and fellow Knight's Cross holder from the *SS-Kavallerie* days, Waldemar. They seen the arrival of American troops into this area, as the surrender came into force, initially working with the Americans to secure the area. The Americans had been sent there to receive the personal surrender of a high-ranking official; that official turned out to the Hermann Göring. With the end of the conflict, Göhler passed into captivity.

This image shows **Reichsmarschall Hermann Göring** as he arrived at a pre-set location to meet American troops.

SS-Ostubaf. **Waldemar Fegelein.**

This formal image shows Hermann Fegelein and his wife Gretl. Fegelein was Göhler's field commander when they were in the *Kavallerie Brigade / Division*, then also later, as Göhler became Fegelein's *Adjutant* at the FHQ.

Besides the many awards listed above, he was also awarded the Wound Badge in Silver and the Close Combat Clasp in Bronze. After his release from being a prisoner of war, he forged a successful post-war career. In his role as Fegelein's Liaison Officer at the Führer Headquarters in 1944, he became acquainted with Otto Günsche and both men struck up a friendship that lasted until their deaths.

During my visit to the *I.Panzer Korps* reunions from 1999 onwards, Göhler was there and in 2000, I had a unique experience that involved this Knight's Cross holder of the *Waffen-SS*. Whilst we awaited the departure of the small land-train that took us to the final night's official evening, I had to return to my room to collect a book to get signed. That act resulted in me missing the land-train leaving, but did put me in the middle of a bizarre situation. Leaving the hotel doors at speed, I inadvertently ran through a group of 5 men standing outside, who were waiting on the land-train. I had the foresight to talk to these men and tell them that they too, had *'missed their lift'*. A quick conversation with one of my travelling companions from the UK, resulted in me offering a lift to some of the men in the group. Those that were there were: Otto Günsche, Hubert Meyer and Johannes Göhler, as well as 2 younger helpers. We quickly realized that 7 people could not fit in the car, so we all decided that I would drive Günsche, Meyer and Göhler, plus one of the helpers, to the event and return for the other 2. That was how I managed to chauffeur 3 well-known and significant former *Waffen-SS* soldiers on a short trip! (As an aside, on the return trip, I performed the same function for Otto Kumm and his wife; this time accompanied by 2 of my UK-based travelling companions.) During that trip with Göhler and Gunsche, their friendship was evident.

Otto Günsche with Adolf Hitler.

Göhler and his wife Ursula.

Peter Mooney and Johannes Göhler in 1999.

Johannes Göhler died on the 21st of February 2003. For me personally, having the chance to get Johannes Göhler to sign a few things, plus talk to him, was welcomed. Having the chance to chauffeur him (and the others) was a pleasant surprise that I will never forget!

Bibliography

Personal correspondence with Johannes Göhler
Waffen-SS Knights and their Battles – Volume 3.
Peter Mooney. *Schiffer Publishing, 2012.*
Personal correspondence between Johannes and Ursula Göhler, 1944-1945, as detailed by David Irving in 1973
Recollections of former American soldier, Lester Leggett, Historynet.com

The Barbarigo Battalion on the Anzio Front
by Massimiliano Afiero – 2nd part

Pennant of *Barbarigo*, Spring 1944.

In March 1944, the *Barbarigo* battalion was transferred to the Anzio bridgehead and located along the sector of the *Grenadier-Regiment 735 (715.Inf.Div.)*, from the section of the Mussolini Canal towards the sea to Borgo Piave, Cerreto Alto and Borgo Sabotino. The marines were immediately engaged in patrol actions and in defensive fighting. On the morning of March 6, when the deployment of the companies was still to be completed, the battalion sustained its first fallen, an eighteen-year-old marine, Alberto Spagna. Facing the *Barbarigo* sector were elements of the *First Special Service Force*, a unit composed of American and Canadian soldiers, well trained as *Rangers*: they immediately attacked the positions of the *Barbarigo*, to assess its resistance. On March 9, during one of their actions, three marines were captured, taken by surprise while carrying a basket of eggs collected in an abandoned hen house.

Towards evening, General Frederick, commander of the Allied unit, having noticed the presence of new enemy units, ordered a new offensive action, attacking the outposts in no man's land. While the strongpoints *Berta* and *Clara* fell into the hands of the enemy, strongpoint *Dora* managed to repel the attack. Seven German soldiers and three Italian sailors were captured in the action. Days of incessant rain followed, which completely halted all activity. During the day, the enemy artillery incessantly hit the Italian-German positions as soon as the Allied observers noticed a slight movement.

Marines of the *Barbarigo* engaged in attacking an enemy strongpoint, March 1944.

A marine of the *Barbarigo* and a German corporal on the Anzio front, 1944.

Marines of the *Barbarigo* armed with MAB submachine gun, during the training at Sezze Romano, March 1944.

The action of the snipers on both sides, forced everyone to remain holed up in their holes full of mud and water. At night, the artillery ceased its activity, and then the patrols, which were going into no man's land, came into action, to place mines, take captives, destroy enemy positions and gather information. The marines continued to be busy reinforcing their positions, without being able to dig holes and deep trenches due to the swampy terrain. During the month of March, patrols continued, which were almost always successful, but which also resulted in losses. Little by little, however, the men of the *Barbarigo* began to earn the respect of the Germans and the enemy. In this same period, the II Company was withdrawn from the first line to be transferred to Sezze: here the *marò* were engaged in a training course to use the *Panzerfaust*, a formidable weapon to stop the numerous Allied tanks engaged in the Lazio bridgehead.

The San Giorgio artillery group

The artillery fire and enemy mortars were constant and the marines could not respond properly. Since their arrival in Sermoneta, the Germans had, however, made it known that they would be able to provide some pieces of Italian artillery seized after September 8th. Vallauri, a former artilleryman, and now the commander of the II Company saw to the preparations and organized the 5th company, of guns, under the orders of S.T.V. Trettene, equipped with four 65/17 pieces from the Museum of Grenadiers. Subsequently, two batteries were created, the 1st on four 105/28 guns and the 2nd on four 105/32 guns. The two batteries that made up the group, would then be called respectively *Speranza* (Hope) and *Fulmine* (Lightning). The artillerymen were taken from the rifle companies, at least sixty marines, chosen by Bardelli himself. On 7 March 1944, the *Barbarigo* batteries were transferred to the front line in the Littoria area. The first (*Speranza*) was initially located south-west of the city, to cover the sector between the sea and Borgo Bainsizza. The second (*Fulmine*) north-west of the town, to cover the upper area of the front. Each had deployed three of its cannons in one place and the fourth in another. This last piece, called the *'phantom piece'*, had the function of attracting enemy fire on itself.

A marine of the *Barbarigo*.

Officers and marines of the *San Giorgio*, March 1944.

Marines of the *San Giorgio* with a 105/23 gun, Spring 1944.

In the following days, the marines began training in the handling and knowledge of artillery pieces, under the control of German officers. At the same time, the construction of the positions for the same batteries was also started, such as pitches, shelters and ammunition depots. On March 12, the first shots were fired, always under the control of German officers. This first phase of training, however, had to be interrupted due to a sudden and massive bombardment of the Allied artillery against the Italian batteries, which caused considerable material and human losses. We listen to the testimony of the Head of 2nd Class, Urbano Medici[1]: "... *In less than no time the first Battery was ready to fire, first target was Borgo Sabotino, at a distance of about 20 km towards the sea"*[2]. In the evening, they told me, 'Tomorrow morning, the order to fire has arrived'. *I checked the level bubbles, I waited for the orders of the section chief Lieutenant Pallastrini:* 'Give the data! Basic piece, three adjustment rounds! Check the convergence! Fire for two hours!'.

Marines of the *San Giorgio* on the Anzio-Nettuno front, March 1944.

A 105/32 gun of the 1st battery of the *San Giorgio*.

It was about nine o'clock in the morning when the 'fire' was finally ordered to the base piece and immediately after the entire Battery began to shoot uninterruptedly. The target was hit repeatedly, even with commendable praise from the German command with a 'Jawohl!'. At about 12:00, the inexperience of a crewman of the 3rd piece was fatal to us. A bullet case remained lodged inside the cannon. The man in charge of loading, to facilitate the expulsion, took it with his hands and, finding it inevitably hot, instinctively threw it away. Unfortunately, the casing fell on the launch charges, placed not far away. These immediately took fire causing very high flames and intense white smoke. At this point it was not

A well-camouflaged gun of the *San Giorgio*, Spring 1944.

Artillery bombardment on the Anzio front, Spring 1944.

difficult for our enemy, the US Navy, to locate our post and start a concentrated fire against us. I remember an officer shouted to leave the pieces line and get into the shelters, but they did not exist yet. I was one of the most experienced, I shouted to the gunners to throw themselves into the holes created by the shellfire, but in moving from one hole to another, by an explosion nearby, I was overwhelmed by a mass of stones and earth".

A marine of the *Barbarigo* in his defensive position, March 1944.

March 1944: marines of the *Barbarigo* engaged in a reconnaissance mission.

Later, the artillerymen were engaged in better camouflaging their firing positions. Through the middle of March, Tenente di Vascello Renato Carnevale came to reinforce, along with some lieutenants from the Artillery and Engineer Academy of Turin and about fifty men. Carnevale assumed command of the group and immediately began the training of the new recruits. Some thought was given to naming The *Barbarigo* artillery group as the '*San Giorgio*', in memory of the cruiser of the same name, however this name was never used, because the artillerymen felt themselves to be an integral part of *Barbarigo*, from which they continued to depend administratively and materially, thus forming the *Barbarigo* Combat Group, comprising both the infantry battalion and the artillery group, integrated into the *Kampfgruppe von Schellerer*: the Italian batteries were tactically integrated into the 1st group of the 671th German artillery regiment.

A patrol of the *Barbarigo* during a mission on the Anzio front, Spring 1944.

First aid is given to a wounded marine, Spring 1944.

The battle continues

On March 14, a platoon of the III Company, under the orders of the GM Mario Cinti, was engaged against an enemy formation. Thanks also to the fire of support of the *San Giorgio* Battery, the attack was repulsed: after firing three hundred rounds and spotted by the enemy, the battery suffered a heavy counter-battery fire. In the night between 17 and 18

March, a mixed Italian-German patrol came into action: the Italian group was under the orders of the GM. Mario Riondino, ex-officer of the Alpini, the Germans were under the orders of a *Feldwebel*. The group advanced in no-man's land, in front of the Strada Lunga, to attack a farmhouse where it was thought there was an enemy observation post. The Italian marines entered the house first, surprising seven American soldiers in their sleep.

A defensive position of the *Barbarigo* on Anzio front, Spring 1944.

Marines medicate a wounded comrade, Spring 1944.

Outside, the sentinel was shot down by a machine gun burst fired by a German soldier: before he died, however, he had time to sound the alarm, firing a flare. Soon after, around the house, Allied artillery shells began to fall, followed by small arms fire. In the midst of that hell of fire and flames were the marines, the German infantrymen and the American prisoners. The German commander, an NCO, was hit by a splinter. His injury caused the group to disperse while the prisoners tried to escape. The GM. Mario Riondino started shooting, hitting two. At that point, the Americans stopped and were brought to the battalion command post. Riondino, even though injured in the foot, managed to bring everyone back. In this regard, let us listen to the testimony of Lieutenant Giulio Cencetti[3]:

Cover of the 'Domenica del Corriere' (March 19, 1944), dedicated to the Barbarigo battalion.

"... *Mortars approached closer, two Germans fall, they all flatten themselves, but get up again: they must run, the prisoners are driven by the shouts of Riondino and of the feldwebel, they also jump on the ground, because the enemy bullets are the same for all, now the group is isolated, a splinter brings down the German NCO:* 'Alt, Stop!' *shouts Riondino. The prisoners who are lying down turn to the rear, they understand amost without seeing each other. Their moment is good for them. Two of them get up. Riondino is small but in a single flash he decides: a burst of fire. The two, hit, do not move anymore. But the submachine gun has jammed. :* I had never killed anyone, I have to bring them to the command post, but what do I do about the NCO?' *No one seems to be in charge anymore: Germans and Italians at odds, everyone is thinking about his own business. Riondino crawls back and reaches the feldwebel An hour ago not he could stand the way the man was, now he cares for him so much and knows he will not let him die like that. He whispers something to convince him. The German understands and extends his hand. A stretched hand, when the blood goes away and one feels dying, always softens. A whisper:* 'Her Leutnant, mein Bruder!', 'Mr. lieutenant, my brother!' *and it was not an entreaty. In the midst of all the firing the prisoners were convinced that the others of the patrol would have cut them down at any hint of escape and they remained still. Mario bends down, does a three-quarter turn and hoists the NCO on his shoulders.* 'How heavy this German is!' *He yells at the prisoners to move. Come on! Not far now to the lines. All hell breaks loose. A sharp pain, like a jiggle in a heel. The load is heavy and the pain is strong. The lieutenant understands that this time they hit him. But everything is still there: a man on his back, running blood and prisoners to take away. He gets there, they get there. He is the last to return. And he takes the prisoners to the command post, as lame as he is. Twenty days later, when he returned from a hospital, where he had been a demon, von Schellerer pinned the Second Class Iron Cross on him that he had earned in the field*".

During one of the following enemy attacks conducted against the front line defended by the III Company, the marines, after having repelled the enemy forces, launched a counterattack and in the fighting that followed the unit commander was wounded, the S.T.V. Honorati. We listen again to Cencetti's testimony[4]: "... *the 3rd Company is attacked strongly. It is a red-hot night, many fall. The foxholesfall apart because of the water that gradually eats away the bottom. Tthe commander is wounded: Lieutenant Honorati, serene, very calm, loses a lot of blood, but everything has to go on. Ruffini, Leoncini and Cinti are doing wonders with the boys of their platoons. Honorati is very pale, but he does not lose control for a moment. Close to him, trying to stop the blood from the wounds, is a second chief student officer ... who urges him to fall back to the infirmary. The lieutenant firmly refuses. There is nothing to do if the situation is not restored, a serious situation that weighs on his young shoulders and on those of the boys who resist with the ardor of little saints and who must follow the example, set by their lieutenant. But the second chief does not want to leave him. Then Honorati, with his good arm, shakes him a little saying: 'Enough. Leave me, move and go to the boys. Some are dying!' And the non-commissioned officer obeys. He obeys twice: because he is his lieutenant and he is also his elder brother. They had enlisted together on the same day".*

Other raids in no man's land were successfully conducted by the 2nd Chief Giuseppe Nicoletti, together with *Feldwebel* Fritz Hassler: every night, the two NCOs led Italian or German patrols, always personally led by them. The patrols had become the patrols led by Fritz und Bepi. On March 18th, on the Mussolini Canal, s.c. Luigi Savelli and the s.c. Luciano Reverdito distinguished themselves. Savelli, after fighting valiantly, was seriously injured in one arm and had to be evacuated in the rear. Reverdito, with his machine gun, he was able to repel an American attack, hitting many of the enemy and forcing others to fall back. Between 19 and 21 March, II Company replaced the III on the front line, becoming subordinated to the I./735. The III Company was transferred to Sezze Romano to be also trained in the use of new anti-tank weapons. On 25 March, the company, located along the Mussolini Canal, was taken over by an Italian SS unit of the 'degli Oddi' battalion, to be transferred to Torre Monticchio for a period of rest and training. But the day after, March 28, the company was split up, to be engaged in guarding the coast between Sabaudia and Terracina. For the sailors a new training cycle given by German instructors began. Also the IV Company, deployed in Fogliano, was heavily engaged in repelling the continuous enemy infiltrations, facilitated by the presence of the forest. In the night between March 30 and April 1, the marines attempted to attack an enemy stronghold: the action was not crowned, however, by success due to the strong enemy resistance and the mixed Italian-German patrol committed suffered one dread and two wounded.

Notes

[1] In "*Come la Fenice*", page 7

[2] The distance is actually about 8 kilometers.

[3] From "*Gli ultimi in grigioverde*", pag. 1083, 1085.

[4] From "*Gli ultimi in grigioverde*", pag. 1085.

Bibliography

Mario Bordogna, "*Junio Valerio Borghese e la X* Flottiglia MAS*", Mursia, Milano, 2007
Guido Bonvicini, "*Decima Marinai! Decima Comandante!*", Mursia, Milano
Daniele Lembo, "*I fantasmi di Nettunia*", Edizioni Settimo Sigillo
Marino Perissinotto, "*Duri a morire - storia del Battaglione Barbarigo*", Ermanno Albertelli
Perissinotto, Panzarasa, "*Come la Fenice*", Editoriale Lupo
Giorgio Pisanò, "*Gli ultimi in grigioverde*", C.D.L. Edizioni

Hungarian Airborne Operation in 1941
By Péter Mujzer

Hungarian paratroopers in full combat kit ready for boarding with Hungarian made reserve and main parachutes, kitbags, weapon bags in 1941.

The lessons learned from the WWI trench war and the idea, how to counter the enemy defence by mobile, airmobile forces by vertical envelopment were understood by the Hungarian military leadership too. The ongoing military conflicts in Spain, Ethiopia and the theoretical and organisational development at the Soviet and German Armies also influenced the top brass to deal with the new kind of warfare. However, sever military condition and financial restriction of the Hungarian Army provided only a modest development of the Hungarian Airborne Troops. In 1938, the Hungarian Ministry of Defence decided to create an airborne infantry force the, "*Ejtőernyős*" (paratroopers). A parachute test centre was established at Szombathely. It was organised by Major Árpád Bertalan, a WWI storm trooper officer, recipient of the highest military decoration of the K. und K. Armee, order of Maria Theresia. Bertalan organised an experimental paratrooper training cadre with seven officer and NCOs. Later 35 and a further 28 NCO and men joined the training unit.

Major Árpád Bertalan.

Caproni Ca-101 was modified for paratrooper training.

Even though parachuting was in it's infancy in 1938, many enthusiastic Hungarian Army infantry NCOs and officers volunteered to join this new unit. Parachutes and other airborne equipment were purchased from all over Europe and from the USA. The Italian *Salvatore* parachute, the German *Schröder* and *Heinecke* parachute, and the US *Irving* parachute were all utilized by the Hungarians. This elite, special unit made many parachute drops with the newly acquired equipment from the antiquated Italian tri engine *Caproni Ca-101* aircraft. Later, in 1939, the Hungarian army developed its own locally-manufactured airborne equipment, knee and elbow pads and a jump smock, as well as the *Hess 39.M* parachute. The Hungarians also updated their aircraft inventory with the *Savoia-Marchetti SM-75*, purchased from Italy, and other modern aircraft.

The first paratrooper traninig cadre in front of a Ca-101 plane.

Paratrooper training, jumping from 2 meters high.

The Hungarian Army Chief of Staff was impressed by the first training exercises of the paratroopers and recognized many practical applications for the new force within the regular army. At the beginning, similar to other countries, two different approaches existed on how to use, organised, equipped and deploy the paratroopers. The Air Force approach was to use small scale, diversionary type paratrooper forces to carry out attacks against dedicated, high profile targets (HQs, bridges, road and railway centres) deep behind the enemy line. This kind of operations needed a highly trained and dedicated troops trained in commando style of warfare. However, the Army needed airmobile infantry to carry out the vertical envelopments in close cooperation and connection with the land forces. This operation needed company/battalion size battle groups reinforced with infantry heavy weapons, anti-tank and light guns. The paratroopers were trained as an elite light infantry force. From the Army point of view the only difference between the infantry and airborne troops was the means of transportation.

Savoia SM-75 transport plane used in 1941.

Hungarian paratroopers, 1941.

Paratrooper NCO in jumping smock with 9mm Bergmann sub-machine gun.

The Hungarian Army Command expanded the paratrooper training program in 1940 and moved its location to the Pápa Airport, where it established a standardized paratrooper school. The troops moved into the old Cavalry Barracks at Pápa.

The Hungarian paratroopers comprised one battalion of three companies with a total nominal strength of 410 men; 30 officers, 120 NCOs, and 250 enlisted men. The 1st Paratrooper Company of the battalion was soon ready for operation in 1941.

The national airline MALERT (Magyar Légiforgalmi R.t.) ceased operations on 16 January 1941, in accordance with the mobilisation plan. The 5 *SIAI-Marchetti SM 75* tri-motor transport planes of the airline were then transferred into the Hungarian Air Force along with their crew and ground personnel and equipment. There, they were formed into the 1st Parachute Transport Squadron and, adding reservists, soon began expansion.

Hungarian paratroopers and a SM-75.

The transport planes worn the E.-101 to 105. identification numbers.

The Balkans Campaign, April 1941.

Paratroopers loading into the SM-75.

April 1941, Voivodina: Hungarian paratroopers used as light infantry transported by trucks.

Invasion of Yugoslavia

The paratroopers were present in the Hungarian OB for the invasion of Yugoslavia, though, by now named 1st Independent Parachute Battalion, and commanded by Major vitéz Arpád Bertalan. In April 1941, the German Army wanted to use Hungary as a jumping off point for their invasion of Yugoslavia. Permission was granted by the Hungarian authorities for the Germans to pass through Hungarian territory to launch their attack. The Hungarian army was indecisive in regarding their role. The Hungarian leadership waited until Croatia, now an autonomous region of Yugoslavia, declared its independence on 10 April 1941. It was used as an excuse to deploy the Hungarian forces in protection of the Hungarian minorities lived on the former Yugoslavian territories, belonged to Hungary before the end of WWI. The Yugoslavian Air Force attacked several times Hungarian targets in connection with the German troop deployments. Yugoslavian planes were shot down by the Hungarian AA artillery and the German fighter planes stationing in Hungary. The Hungarian troops started to invade Voivodina (Bácska) on 11 April 1941. The Hungarian parachute battalion was placed on alert for possible deployment and kept in reserve by the Hungarian 3rd Army (commanded by Colonel General Elemér Novák). When the Hungarians attacked from the north, the Yugoslav troops retreated from their first defensive line along the border with Hungary, behind the Franz Josef Canal. The Canal divides the Bácska area and the two canal bridges at Szenttamás and Verebszász had to be taken before the Hungarian Mobile Corps (Commanded by Major General Béla Miklós) could occupy the rest of the region.

Left Photo: paratrooper with Hungarian invented drop container on wheel to make the delivery easier. Right Photo: Hungarian paratrooper in full combat kit with submachine gun in canvas cover, main and spare parachutes.

Hungarian paratroopers in firing position with 20mm anti-tank rifle and *Bergmann* sub-machine guns.

Royal Hungarian Army Parachutist Badge.

The Hungarian Parachute Battalion was to be dropped behind this line, approach the bridges from the rear, and seize them. On April 12, 1941 the Hungarian Paratroopers prepared for their first combat jump. The rainy spring weather marked the whole operation during the Yugoslavian Campaign, which hampered the land and air activities as well as. The empty transport aircrafts flew over to Veszprém Air Field, to which operations had been shifted because rain had left the runway at Pápa Airport, composed of compressed dirt and gravel, too muddy for use. The airfield at Veszprém was the only military air base with a cement runway, so it was used by the paratroopers that day for the airborne assault on

Yugoslavia. The reinforced 1st Paratrooper Company and their equipment were transported by trucks to the airport. The plane was to drop about 200 men in two separated waves to the target area. The first wave consisted of 4 transport plane carrying 4x22 paratroopers and their equipment in drop canisters fixed in the load compartments of the SM-75 planes. The four planes should fly in rhomboid formation and drop the paratroopers within 60 seconds over the double bridge of Újverebszász on the afternoon of 12 April to capture the bridges and dismantle the demolition charges and prevent the destruction of the vital communication junction. The second wave would drop on the morning of 13 April to reinforce the defence of the bridges until the arrival of the mobile forces. The take-off was ordered at 17.00 hours of 12 April 1941.

Hungarian camouflaged SM-75 'E.103'.

Árpád Bertalan as a Captain in the Hungarian Army.

The E.101 was piloted by Captain László Kelemen the commander of the Transport Squadron, Major Árpád Bertalan the commander of the 1st Independent Paratrooper Battalion set behind him on the plane. The E.101 started its take off, everything went in order, E.103 was behind it to start the take-off, while E.103 taxying to the starting point and E.104 prepared for taxying. When suddenly the E.101 started to climb steeply, lost its power and crashed into the ground. The engines worked until the impact, the plane was full of aviation fuel which exploded almost immediately. By miracle seven men survived the crash, one airman and six paratroopers. The ground crew and the paratroopers of the second wave started the rescue, but the exploding ammunition and fuel did not allow them to the plane to evacuate the wounded survivors. The operation was stopped and the accident reported to the Army Command. The second in command Captain Imre Majthényi survived the crash, but wounded, so the command was taken over by 1st Lieutenant Zoltán Kiss, he recommended carrying on with the operation from military and psychological point of views too. The paratroopers were shocked and lethargic due to the accident. 1st Lieutenant Kiss recommended executing the mission with three transport planes and two drops and a slightly reduced numbers and loads. That time the cause of the accident was unknown. The dead toll of the accident were 16 paratroopers and four Air Force personal, seven men survived, two men died in the hospital due to severe burns. Another four could get out the plane but were engulfed by the flames and burned to die.

Hungarian paratrooper company on parade in jumping smock and helmet.

At 19.00 hours the order arrived for take-off. The three SM-75 took-off and headed to the target area. However the E.102 lagged behind for engine failures, but they continued. The detailed maps were lost with the crashed SM-75 it made the navigation difficult. The first two planes dropped their paratroopers three minutes before the drop zone at the height of 200 meters. The last plane dropped its paratroopers, when they saw the withe canopies already on the drop zone. The paratroopers landed 15 kilometres away from the planned target, and clashed with Serbian forces around a farm house lost two men killed and three wounded. Later the paratroopers joined the units of the Mobile Corps. The second wave was cancelled. The 2nd Paratrooper Company was deployed by truck to the operation. The investigation finally came to the conclusion that mechanical failure caused the deadly plane crash, which could be rooted in the improper winter storage of the SM-75 transport planes. As the Germans noted the paratrooper commanders should take off with the last plane but had to jump first over the target. This proved to be the last combat drop done by Hungarian paratroopers during the WWII. In 5 July of 1941, the Transport Squadron carried out a supply drop over the Carpathian Mountains in support of the land forces, during the *Barbarossa* Campaign. A selected group of 9 paratroopers escorted and jumped with the canisters to recover them after the mission.

Bibliography

Horváth Csaba – Lengyel Ferenc, "*A délvidéki hadművelet, 1941. április*", Puedlo

Dr. Lengyel, "*A 3. Magyar Királyi Hadsereg délvidéki hadműveletei*", ZMNK

Leo Niehorster, "*The Royal Hungarian Army 1920-45*", Bayside Books, 1998

Reszegi Zsolt, "*Légi huszárok, Az ejtőernyős csapatnem kialakulása és harcai 1938 és 1945 között*", 2013 Budapest-Pápa

Huszár János, "*Honvéd Ejtőernyősök Pápán 1938-1945*", 1999 Jókai Kör

Levegőből harcba, "*A magyar katonai ejtőernyőzés története és változó feladatrendszere*", 2013 Zrínyi kiadó

Turcsányi Károly – Hegedűs Ernő, "*A légideszant I. Elmélet, eljárások és a légi gépesítés a kezdetektől 1945-ig*"

The last battle of the Charlemagne Division
by Tomasz Borowski

Waffen-Rottenführer **Robert Soulat was a precious witness of the *'Charlemagne'* Division's history. He was not sent to Berlin, and was captured in Mecklenburg by the British Army on 3 May 1945.**

SS-Brigadeführer **Krukenberg, Inspector of the *'Charlemagne'* and commander of the *'Nordland'* during the Battle of Berlin.**

Rebuilding after defeat in Pomerania

On 8 March, around 200 people arrived in the town of Anklam. They were members of the divisional staff company, auxiliary units and the Honour Guard. Every day saw more and more survivors flock to the rendezvous point. The staff found their quarters in a room in a large country residence, which was crowded with refugees. The unit's administration duties were performed at two tables situated by the window. Refugees and soldiers alike had to camp there day and night, so the SS men decided to make themselves straw beds under the huge pool table that stood in the corridor. When *Waffen-Rottenführer* Soulat went to get the straw for himself, he was stopped by the owner of the residence, who forbade him from taking anything. Soulat was furious. Wasn't he here to fight for Germany and all of Europe? He bellowed at the German, who responded in kind but after a moment he turned on his heel and walked away. Soulat informed him that when the Russians came, they wouldn't ask for permission and would be perfectly able to take care of everything themselves[1].

SS-Brigadeführer Krukenberg arrived on 16 March, alongside 23 other officers and a group of 700 soldiers of the 'Fenet' Battalion. Two days later, on 18 March, Krukenberg visited *Reichsführer-SS* Himmler's headquarters near Prenzlau to report on *'Charlemagne'* Division's actions during the fighting in Pomerania. Upon his return the next day, in recognition of their service, he awarded medals and promotions to many soldiers who emerged from the huge loss of life that took place the previous month. *Waffen-Rottenführer* Soulat pointed out in his memoirs that it was the first time their commander wore the écusson tricolore on his jacket – a shield in French national colours. During the ceremony, Henri Fenet received promotion to *Waffen-Hauptsturmführer* for his singular heroism and peerless courage. Fenet's aide, Labourdette, was promoted from the rank of *Waffen-Standartenoberjunker* to *Waffen-Untersturmführer*.

Immediately afterwards, the newly promoted Labourdette received the Iron Cross 1st Class, and *Waffen-Untersturmführer* Martres – with 15 other soldiers –the Iron Cross 2nd Class. In many cases, the orders had to be awarded posthumously. In the following weeks, many more of the French volunteers were recognized for their tremendous valour.

Henri Fenet, to left, with other French SS volunteers, during a permission in January 1944.

Waffen-Ustuf. Jean Labourdette was the commanding officer of the 1st Company of the *'Charlemagne'* battalion in Berlin.

Jean-Marie Croisile was in charge of one platoon of the 1st Company in Berlin. Wounded, he was able to escape before the fall of the city.

During that time, one of those volunteers, Jean-Marie Croisile, reflected on the past few weeks: *"As for me, I feel sadness when I think of all those who fell, my colleagues and my superiors alike: Wagner, Walter, Obitz, Merlat, Denamps and all those many many others … How many of us is left of the eight or nine thousand soldiers of the Charlemagne that decamped from Wildflecken? And I wonder also about the boys I sent out for the Russian front back in June, 1943, when I was still just a machine gunner. How many of them still live? And I wonder if I'm not the only one … For the time being, anyway. Perhaps not for long!"*[2].

On 21 March, the French grouped at Anklam train station, from where they were to travel to their new quarters in Mecklenburg. None of the trains arrived, however, so the French had to make their way on foot. The soldiers amused themselves with song as they marched. They spent the night in the village of Schwerinsburg and moved on at dawn. They marched through Samow, then Friedland, where they split into small groups to find shelter in surrounding buildings. The Staff Company spent the night in a school in Schonbeck. Next day, 23 March, started well for everyone. The soldiers got milk for their breakfast, a beverage they hadn't had the opportunity to taste in quite some time. They moved out again. In the evening, after having walked for over 20km, the unit made camp in Stolpe, where they were able to enjoy a potato feast they prepared themselves, troubled by no-one. On 24 March, the formation arrived near Neustrelitz, where they made their quarters in the surrounding villages. The staff chose a castle in Carpin. It turned out to be a castle in name only as, upon arrival, they saw simply a large residence. It was the only house in the area, however, equipped with electricity, which was an absolute treat[3].

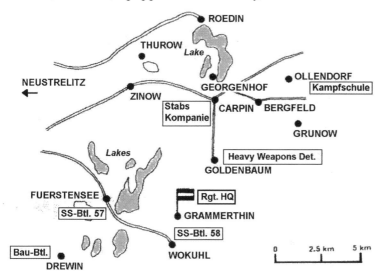 

SS-Rgt. 'Charlemagne' reformation Area, East-Southeast of Neustrelitz, March-April 1945.

Waffen-Sturmbannführer Boudet-Gheusi.

Walter Zimmermann.

On Sunday, 25 March, delousing was called. Later that day, an order came from *SS-Führungshauptamt* (SS Head Office) to reform the *Waffen-Grenadier Division der SS 'Charlemagne'* into a Grenadier Regiment, structurally based on the 'Type 1945' Infantry Division. The order, which was to take effect on 15 April, did not dissolve the unit, but incorporated it (at least in theory) into the 3rd Panzer Army from Vistula Army Group. *SS-Brigadeführer* Krukenberg, as Inspector for the 'Charlemagne' Division, decided to leave the command of the new formation (which was to be henceforth known as *Waffen-Grenadier Regiment der SS 'Charlemagne'*) in the hands of its previous CO, *SS-Standartenführer* Zimmermann. The regiment comprised three battalions: *57.SS-Bataillon* under the command of *Waffen-Hauptsturmführer* Fenet; *58. SS-Bataillon* under *Waffen-Obersturmführer* Geromini; and *Schwere Bataillon* under *Waffen-Sturmbannführer* Boudet-Gheusi[(4)]. The core of the *57.Bataillon* consisted of the old regiment of the same designation. It could be considered a successor of the old French SS-Assault Brigade. All her veterans, who managed to survive the bloody fighting in Galicia and the hell of Pomerania, served in the unit, including Henri Fenet. The *58.Bataillon* was also an extension of that same regiment.

French SS volunteers captured in Pomerania by Polish soldiers, March 1945.

Wilhelm Weber, here in *SS-Untersturmführer* rank.

The morale of her old legionnaires from the LVF and the militants of the Miliciens was not as high as that of those from the 57th. The trial by fire that those former members of the Milice Française went through in Pomerania left a lasting mark. The battalion's commander, Geromini, had a very difficult, if not impossible, task before him to encourage his men to regain their fighting spirit for a cause practically as good as lost. The most elite part of the Charlemagne Regiment, the 40-strong Compagnie d'Honneur (Honour Guard), was directed to the village of Georgenhof, north of Carpin. Its commander was the still young but battle-tested *SS-Obersturmführer* Wilhelm Weber. He immediately enacted his fierce training regiment[(5)]. In the meantime, an increasing number of French volunteers kept arriving in Carpin. Some of them were survivors, other were graduates of various training programmes and courses, who were spared the fighting their original division went through in Pomerania. Among them was also a large group of brand new recruits who were hoping that being on the front line would be better than staying in German cities, still in danger from Allied carpet bombings. Some of them foolishly believed that as soldiers of the *Waffen SS*, they would enjoy better food and living conditions than as civilians. Their hopes were soon disappointed. It may be considered as a curious but inexplicable fact that some of the '*Charlemagne*' survivors who lived through the battle for Kołobrzeg, were sent through Świnoujście not to Carpin but to Wildflecken, a couple of hundred kilometres further, where the French *Ausbildungs-und-Ersatz Bataillon* (Auxiliary-Training Battalion) was stationed. The number of troops amassing in Carpin kept growing steadily until they became too many for their quarters.

March 1945, German soldiers engaged in building a defensive position on the Oder front.

German anti-tanks unit on bycicle and *Panzerfaust*.

A German defensive position, March 1945.

As a result, some of the company had to camp in towns further away from the command post. Eventually, a hastened military training could begin, but the fragile morale of some of the soldiers did not help and caused unit cohesion to be a problem. The former Francs-gardes lost their heart for continued service, giving voice to their bitterness during a fight with German personnel. Veterans of the SS-Assault Brigade took part in the confrontation, with both sides throwing accusations at each other. In the meantime, at the beginning of April, a group of *Wehrmacht* officers, led by *Oberst* von Massow, were scouting the Neustrelitz region to prepare defensive positions before the expected assault by the Red Army.

Sappers laying Teller mines during a defensive action in March 1945.

Waffen-Oscha. **François Appolot.**

The French SS were ordered to build fortifications and dig anti-tank ditches. This belittling order was not met with enthusiasm. *Waffen-Hauptsturmführer* Fenet also found it demoralizing, but did not let it show. He realized that an order was an order and had to be carried out, and so he worked like everybody else. He knew that actions meant more than words. When dawn came and the day of work was to begin, he showed up with a group of his men, took off his shirt and asked for a shovel: he was first to start to dig. He worked alone in silence for a while before – one by one – his men followed his example[6]. Insubordination was a continuous issue, despite the fact that even the smallest infraction was severely punished. By order of the *Führer* himself, every deserter, thief or looter was to be put to death. To make sure each of his men was familiar with that order, Fenet made every one of them sign it. A few days later, a worried *Waffen-Untersturmführer* Labourdette reported to Fenet a case of petty theft. One of the farmers made a complaint that French NCOs staying in his home stole a few light bulbs. A quick investigation revealed the guilty parties and brought them before the battalion's CO, *Waffen-Hauptsturmführer* Fenet. Aware of the consequences of their actions, the perpetrators expected to be executed. Fenet, however, simply admonished them thoroughly. Not all were so lucky, however. Having refused the order to dig the antitank ditches, one of the regiment commanders, *Waffen-Untersturmführer* Emile Gerard, was accused of abandoning his post during the battle for Elsenau (Olszanowo) at the end of February, even though the matter was not addressed at the time. The court martial found Gerard guilty and sentenced him to death. The firing squad, led by *Waffen-Oberscharführer* François Appolot, was formed out of members of the Honour Guard. Gerard was shot on the night of 19 April at the Carpin cemetery. Another instance of insubordination in the ranks of the French volunteers was the arrest of two deserters who were found dressed as civilians in Berlin. They were moved to desertion by a Belgian woman they both lived with for a while. The two soldiers were *Waffen-Sturmmann* Turco and *Waffen-Grenadier* Harel. The first was a veteran of the French *SS-Sturmbrigade* and fought in Galicia in the ranks of the 1.Bataillon. In Fenet's eyes, that made him even more guilty than Harel, who was previously affiliated with the *Kriegsmarine*. Both men faced a court martial chaired by *Waffen-Sturmbannführer* Boudet-Gheusi. The court found them guilty, yet did not condemn them to death as instructed by the order of the *Führer*. Having learned of this, Gustav Krukenberg flew into a rage. As far as he was concerned, the deserters were either guilty and deserved the ultimate punishment, or they were not and should be exonerated and set free. Any other possibility should not have been considered. Both rulings were thus annulled and the cases retried. The chairmanship of the court martial this time went to *Waffen-Untersturmführer* Labourdette of the *57.Bataillon*. This time the deserters were sentenced to death by firing squad: the judgement was passed on 12 April and execution was set for the next morning....

SS-Brigadeführer **Krukenberg.**

I want only true warriors with me

In early April 1945, the headcount of the *'Charlemagne'* Regiment rose to about 1,000 soldiers. *Reichsführer-SS* Himmler and *SS-Brigadeführer* Krukenberg made the decision to restructure the unit and separate those who were willing to continue fighting from those who were not. The latter were to be assigned to the so called *Bau-bataillon* (construction battalion). Gustav Krukenberg called the men to assembly to give a small speech, which went as follows: *"Those who don't wish to fight any more will remain in the SS but they will work as builders. In our continued fight I want only volunteers. I want only true warriors with me"*. For the men from the Honour Guard there was only one obvious choice: fight until the end. One of them, *Waffen-Unterscharführer* Puechlong, stated that since he had sworn fielty, he would remain true to his oath. His comrade, Louis Levast, wrote a letter to Robert Forbes in which he confessed: *"Even though we were aware the war was lost, we decided to fight on and not to get captured alive by [the] Russians. We also naively hoped that in the last moment the new, wonderful* Wunderwaffe [miracle weapon] *would come"*[7].

In the end, 75 percent of the men from Fenet's battalion and 50 percent of those from Geromini's battalion chose guns over pickaxes and shovels. The mindset of those who chose to remain was perfectly shown by *SS-Rottenführer* Robert Soulat. He believed that it would be shameful to give up now that so many of his friends had already given their lives in Pomerania. Were they aware that in time, they would be condemned and cursed?[8]. The Construction Battalion gained one officer and about 400 NCOs and privates.

German soldiers get ready to fight.

LVF-Jagdkommando. On the left is *Waffen-Hscha.* Pierre Rostaing.

German defensive position, March 1945.

The majority of those came from the ranks of the Milice Française and LVF. They believed that to continue to fight the unwinnable war was delusional. Gustav Krukenberg placed the charge of this ephemeral formation into the hands of *Waffen-Hauptsturmführer* Roy, who did not shy away from expressing his disappointment in his commander's decision. He wanted to fight on. Krukenberg, however, needed trusted officers in the battalion, and Roy was one of them. The units were stationed in separate locations, and from that point on had practically no contact with each other.

In the meantime, on 10 April, the survivors from the Marching Battalion arrived. During the Pomeranian calamity that befell the 'Charlemagne' Division, this battalion had fought near Gotenhafen (Gdynia). The majority of these soldiers, including a number of the wounded and those with frostbite, signed up for the *57.* and *58.Bataillon* and declared their wish to remain in action. In the following days, the *58.Bataillon* changed its CO. Geromini, charged with spreading defeatism, was relieved of his duty and replaced by *Waffen-Hauptsturmführer* Jauss. Those who volunteered to continue to fight were made to renew their oath of fealty to the *Führer* until death. For many of them, it was already a third oath since their joining the German Army. One of those volunteers, *Waffen-Hauptscharführer* Pierre Rostaing, mentioned in his post-war memoirs that he wasn't even a national socialist. He was only driven to fight communism, which he believed to be *"the enemy of all civilization"*[9]. Ultimately, the *57.Bataillon*, showing the highest morale, was stationed in Furtensee. Its complement was as follows:

CO, *Waffen-Hauptsturmführer* Fenet;
1.*Kompanie, Waffen-Ustuf.* Labourdette;
2.*Kompanie, Waffen-Hauptscharführer* Hennecart;
3.*Kompanie,* CO unknown;
4.*Kompanie, Waffen-Oberscharführer* Ollivier.

The number of soldiers in the *58.Bataillon* diminished significantly, but the selection process brought the result desired by Krukenberg. It was comprised of the toughest, most experienced veterans of the LVF, full of energy and the will to fight. Many of them had served on the Eastern Front ever since the beginning of the first winter of the Legion in 1941/42. The unit's structure was as follows:

CO, *SS-Hauptsturmführer* Jauss;
5.Kompanie, Waffen-Standartenjunker Aumon;
6.Kompanie, Waffen-Hauptsturmführer Rostaing;
7.Kompanie, Waffen-Obersturmführer Fatin;
8.Kompanie, Waffen-Untersturmführer Sarailhe[10]

Waffen-Oberscharführer Jean Ollivier was the commanding officer of the 4th company.

The new battalion CO, *SS-Hauptsturmführer* Jauss, unfortunately was not the same soldier who, in cooperation with Fenet, led his men out of the encirclement during their retreat to Dziwnów [Dievenow]. Overwhelmed and disappointed by the situation he was in, he became quiet and withdrawn. Two of his company leaders, however, Rostaing and Fatin, were able to keep the battalion together with their charisma. The *57.Bataillon* was led by the Honour Guard, comprised of some 80 men. During the restructuring it was renamed as *Kampfschule*. Weber's boys (Weber was the company's leader) laughed out loud when they were asked if they wanted to be reassigned to the rear. They were proud and fanatical, believing themselves to be the elite of the entire *'Charlemagne'* Division. As proof, they were the first to acquire their camouflage uniforms[11]. These soldiers became the heroes of an interesting story, which reflects the spirit of the unit. The incident in question took place during one of the morning musters, in the middle of April, when the entire *Kampfschule* stood on parade in front of the officer from the German Inspectors.

Belt buckle with inscription '*Gott Mit Uns*'.

SS belt buckle with '*Meine Ehre heißt Treue*'.

The soldiers were missing their belts and buckles on their uniform jackets. It is not hard to imagine the confusion amongst the Germans, unaccustomed to such insubordination as they were. When called to report, *SS-Obersturmführer* Weber explained with infinite poise that his men had received only *Wehrmacht* buckles with the inscription *'Gott mit uns'* ('God is with us'), which was obviously ill-fit for the men of the SS! As an afterthought, he added that they did not need any God. Perplexed, the German staff officer was speechless. Soon thereafter, the battalion was supplied with buckles bearing the *Waffen-SS* motto *'Meine ehre heisst treue'* ('Fielty is my honour').

Waffen SS officer, April 1945.

German soldiers in a railway station, April 1945.

Waffen-Obersturmführer Michel.

Meanwhile, the command was impatiently awaiting the arrival of 1,200 French SS. Led by *SS-Obersturmbannführer* Hersche, they were to make their way on foot from their camp in Wildflecken on the night of 30 March. Regrettably, there was no news on their progress. Command was also waiting for the Assault Gun Company that was in training in Moravia in the Czech Republic. On 14 April, some 20 French officer candidates rejoined their unit in Carpin. They completed their training at the *SS-Panzer-Grenadier-Schule Kienschlag* in Neveklov [Neweklau] in the Czech Republic. The course hardened their bodies and minds, now filled with fanaticism and willingness for sacrifice. The arrival of those officers greatly improved the combat spirit of the entire formation. Their thirst for the fight, however, had to be curbed for the time being. The Assault Gun Company finally arrived. It was originally equipped with *Jagdpanzer 38(t) Hetzer* assault guns. These were, however, confiscated by Army Group Centre, under Field Marshal Ferdinand Schoerner's command. As a result, these soldiers could still fight, but only as common grenadiers[12]. Soon after the new senior officers were integrated into the '*Charlemagne*' Regiment, Neustrelitz saw the arrival of one of the former division instructors, *Waffen-Obersturmführer* Michel. As a member of the training personnel, he was assigned to the aforementioned *SS-Panzer-Grenadier-Schule Kienschlag*. The *57.Bataillon* CO, Henri Fenet, gave him the command of the *2.Kompanie*, whose former leader, *Waffen-Hauptscharführer* Hennecart, was reassigned to the Regiment HQ. Meanwhile, *SS-Hauptsturmführer* Jauss, the young CO of the *58.Bataillon*, became increasingly disillusioned and demotivated in his leadership of his men. *SS-Brigadeführer* Krukenberg could not tolerate such an attitude: he had to protect that incredible combat spirit amongst his 700 volunteers. In his report to the *SS-Fuhrungshauptamt* (SS-FHA), he stated: "*SS-Hauptsturmführer Jauss should no longer be with the French volunteers. He would, however, be an exemplary leader in the SS cadet school*". This was tantamount to a request for Jauss's reassignment, which indeed took place soon thereafter.

This article is an extract from the book "*The price of the oath: the French ss Sturmbataillon during the battle of Berlin 1945*", by Tomasz Borowski. The book is available directly from the author in e-book format. Price for complete book (250 pages main book + plus two colour sections and big Berlin map) is 7 GBP / 8 EUR. Paypal accepted. For more info: tobor2@wp.pl.

Notes

[1] Forbes, Robert, "*For Europe. French Volunteers of the Waffen SS*". Helion & Company, 2006.

[2] Fenet, Henri, "Berlin, derniers témoignages", Editions de l'Homme Libre, 2014, ch: Jean-Marie Croisile. Berliner Verteidig, pp.241-79.

[3] Forbes, Robert, op.cit.

[4] Ibid.

[5] Ibid.

[6] Ibid.

[7] Ibid.

[8] Lefèvre, Eric, "*Les volontaires de l'apocalypse*", Uniformes, No.300, 2015.

[9] Forbes, Robert, op.cit.

[10] Ibid.

[11] Two-part Erbsterntarn camouflage uniforms.

[12] Forbes, Robert, op.cit.

SS-Hauptsturmfuhrer Hans-Jörg Hartmann
III Batl. 'Nordland' regiment 5th SS division "Wiking

By Ken Niewiarowicz – 3rd part

This is a photo-essay based on a stack of Photo albums and documents from the estate of *SS-Hstuf.* Hans-Jörg Hartmann, born in Berlin-Licterfeld on October 21, 1913. The associated text is drawn from the captions of the photos as well as information in the documents that are associated with this grouping. The following photographs are in chronological order as they appear in the 2 wartime photo albums, compiled from photographs Hartmann between June and November 1941, while commanding 12th company in the campaign in the Ukraine.

On the north Rollbahn at Radomischel.

SS-Hstuf. Erich Rosenbusch, 9th Kompanie commander.

4 weeks since the beginning of regiment Nordland's offensive, in the vicinity of Cherkassy; half way through the Ukraine.

Difficult road conditions after heavy rain.

The Ukrainian mud seems bottomless.

Hartmann describes the conditions: "*And in sunshine, dust and thirst are constant companions*".

in World War Two 1939-1945

23-28 July 1941 Luka-Boguslav. DKW 350 motorcycles.

Wiking Division headquarters. *Sdkfz* 222 vehicles and *Horch* command vehicles.

Sturmgeschütz and other *Wiking* vehicles.

A German *PzKpfw.III* on the Eastern front, Summer 1941.

Left photo, German Panzer. Right photo: Like many SS officers in this period, Hartmann has adopted the practice of removing his collar insignia. Note also the non-regulation wear of an Army officer side cap with a metal SS skull applied to the front.

The Battalion commander confers with company officers in front of Boguslav.

SS-Sturmbannfuhrer Blöw (commander *III./Nordland*) against the backdrop of the plains of north central Ukraine; rolling hills and grasslands interspersed by ravines and crevasses.

Rare front-line shot of advancing German armor.

in World War Two 1939-1945

A German *PzKpfw.IV* on Eastern front, Summer 1941.

A *Fiesler Storch* observation airplane joins the attack.

Knight's cross winner *SS-Oberführer* Fritz von Scholtz, Commander of regiment *Nordland*.

SS-Oscha. Mery, Third platoon leader of Hartmann's company.

Hartmann captions this photo: "*The face of the German infantryman*".

Dismounted from the vehicles and resting near Kremenchuk.

Hartmann in a *Horch* command car.

A BMW R12 motorcycle and sidecar.

(To be continued)

Dutch Legion Awards
by Rene Chavez

Anton Mussert.

Dutch NSB Awards

The Dutch NSB Party under Anton Mussert produced and issued many awards to legion volunteers and party members. One of the most recognizable and prestigious awards is the so-called Mussert Cross.

The Mussert Bravery Cross

The Dutch Nazi Party "NSB" under the leadership of Anton Mussert instituted a special award for NSB members in German service. This Dutch made award commonly known as the "Mussertkruis" (Mussert Cross). The "NSB" political party referred the award as the "Oostlanderskruis" and it was most likely equivalent of the German Eastern Front Medal, it was not as previously thought as a bravery award. It comes in two classes; with swords for combatants and without swords (very rare) for non-combatants. The cross is made of three parts from enamel and high quality gilt finished metal. The outside edge of the cross is in black enamel on both sides with inner portion finished in translucent red.

The Mussert Bravery Cross (*Rene Chavez Collection*).

A separate white disc is soldered to the front and back of the cross. The front side shows gilt wolf hook over swastika with oak leaves. The back side shows around the top edge of the circle the motto of the NSB in gilt "*Hou En Trou*" and oak leaves on the bottom edge. The center of the disc has the name "*MUSSERT*" and date "*1941*". The ribbon shows the Dutch National Colors. The ribbon colors are sky blue, white with thin orange strip to the center, white and sky blue. The award came in a two piece maroon outer card case. The award was probably worn eventhough it was not authorized to be worn on German uniform. According to some sources, the medal was manufactured by the *National Mint* in Utrecht.

Above is a nice rare example of the Mussert Cross, ribbon bar and case. The award and ribbon bar are placed in a cardboard case of maroon color with golden stripes. The interior is covered in burgundy velvet (*Rene Chavez Collection*).

Mussert Memorial Plaque

The "Mussert plaquette" (Mussert Plaque), also referred as "*Eastern Front*" Plaque, were issued to family members to commemorate or honor those volunteers who fell in action on the Eastern Front. There is a possibility that these plaques were presented with a certificate.

The plaques were etched on a plain surface made of zinc. The size is approx. 67mm by 41mm. These plaques were presented in a plain, black cardboard box lined with purple velvet. These plaques are very rare and only less than 20 are found in collections.

On the left, the "Mussert plaquette" for the Dutch volunteer J.L. Persainere (*Rene Chavez Collection*).

W.A. Military Sports Badge

The "*WeerbaarheidsAfdeling*" (Defense Sections) were the Storm troopers of the NSB. Military sporting events were held for W.A. troops and successful winners were awarded with the military sport badge. The sport badge shows in the background a Laurel with the NSB emblem "*wolf hook*" in front. The reverse is hollow with two small loop rings that holds the pin. This die stamped badge was awarded in two classes, silver and bronze gilt. Badge shown below is Gilt class. The badge is very large it measures 53mm in diameter. It was instituted on 13 September 1941.

W.A. Military Sports Badge.

A W.A. member with the Sports Badge.

The Dutch NSKK Honor Badge

New information has surface in regards to Dutch volunteers who served in the "NSKK" German Motorized Transport service. It was to be bestowed upon those persons who showed exceptional service in the Motor W.A. The volunteers in the Dutch NSKK could also be awarded the honour badge if they showed great Courage, Loyalty and Fidelity. It was made in three classes: Bronze, Silver and Gold. The inspector of the Motor W.A, Banleader Eman, made the decisions on who was to be awarded one of the classes, but only after consulting the leading liaison officer at the *NSKK-Gruppe Luftwaffe*. The rendering of the badge took place twice a year in the case of the bronze: on the 11th of May and the 9th of November. In between these dates a person could only be awarded one of the badges in very particular cases and in exceptional circumstances. For example in the case of the silver class, Banleader Eman decided that this grade was only to be awarded in very exceptional cases hence the rarity of the badge. The badge is die struck and is made of an alloy composed of bronze-copper. In the front center it shows the Dutch party emblem "wolf-hook" with a German helmet on the left side and a sword facing down on the right side. On the background it shows a transport tire with an inscription "TROUW" (Loyalty) on top. The hollow back shows a Belgium style "C" catch and thin Belgium style pin.

Dutch volunteers in the N.S.K.K. They wear *Luftwaffe* uniform with N.S.K.K. collar patches and shoulder straps. They wear as their "*national badge*", the arm badge of the W.A.

Dutch NSKK Honor Badge.

The badge measures 46.8mm x 51.2mm. Also recent information has surface thanks to my Dutch colleague Alex Dekker who is currently writing a book on Dutch Volunteers and has kindly provided the following information taken from his book. According to the Dutch published NSKK-paper *'Alles sal reg kom 1e jaargang, extra nummer November 1943'* the following qualifications for the bronze class are:

1. For those who served in the winter of 1941-1942, from November continuously for 6 months in Russia. The persons that were also entitled to the German "*Winterschlacht*" (Eastern Front) medal.

2. The men who were wounded during service in the battle for Milorowo, wearers of the German "*Verwundetenabzeichen*" (wounded badge).

3.The men who applied voluntary for "*wachtkommando*" (Guard-Duties) in Makajewka.

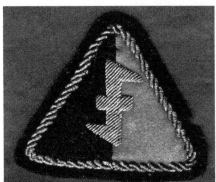

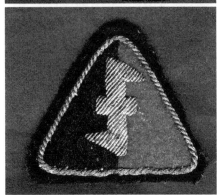

Dutch recruiting poster for the NSKK.

The Loyalty badge in Silver was to be awarded only in Christmas. The names of the persons who were considered for the award were submitted for approval to the Dutch liaison Staff. The Gold class seems not to have been awarded, however, the criteria for this grade are not known. Those who think that they deserve the medal, should apply at the staff offices located in Brussels, Belgium and Utrecht, Holland. Miloworo and Makajewka were key-cities during siege for Stalingrad and in both these cities the NSKK had to provide ammunition and food for the 6th Army (which was supplied by air) and the armies who had to break open the Kessel. It should be noted that good reproductions of this badge have surface, they are cast and have different attaching hardware shown on the reverse.

Dutch NSKK Insignia

Most of the Dutch NSKK volunteers came under the control of the German Luftwaffe. The Dutch NSKK saw active service in the Eastern Front as the "NSKK Regiment Niederlande."According to Littlejohn's book, volume 2 of Foreign Legions of the Third Reich; Dutch NSKK troops took more then a thousand Russian prisoners and were awarded with twenty five Iron Crosses. It interesting to note that several hundred Dutch NSKK men fought under the German 6th Army at Stalingrad. These men were attached to the "*NSKK Transportgruppe Luftwaffe 2.Brig/2.Bat./6.Regiment*". Only 50 came out of the Kessel and it is believe that all were decorated with the NSKK badge.

Illustrated to left, is a Dutch arm shield and headgear that is normally associated to the "*Weer Afdeelingen* (W.A.)" storm troopers of the N.S.B. However, this insignia with the gold embroidered wolf hook and border was also issued and worn by Dutch NSKK volunteers whether they were ex-N.S.B. members or not.

WW2 AXIS
FORCES

Made in the USA
Middletown, DE
17 February 2020